Sk8 for Jake

Written by
Rob Waring and **Maurice Jamall**

Before You Read

to fly

to jump

to skate

bench

phone

poster

sk8 = sk(eight) = skate

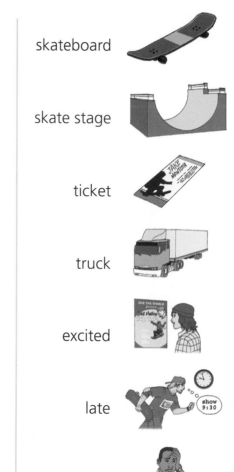

skateboard

skate stage

ticket

truck

excited

late

worried

"Look at me," says John. "I'm flying!" John is jumping with his skateboard. John, Eric, and Yoko are skating in the park. They are good skateboarders.

"Wow, John, that's great," says Eric.

"Watch this," says Yoko. She jumps over the bench with her skateboard.

A man comes to them. He is Mr. Walker and he works in the park. Mr. Walker is angry. "Stop that!" he says. "Do not play on the benches!"

Yoko says, "But we like skating here, Mr. Walker."

Mr. Walker says, "The benches are for people, not for skateboards. No skating here. Go away."

Yoko, John, and Eric are in town. They have their skateboards, but they are not happy. They want to skate in the park. Yoko sees a poster. She runs to it. "Hey!" says Yoko. "Come and look at this!"
Eric and John go over to Yoko.

She shows them the poster. "Wow!" they say. "Look, it's *Jake Montoya and his Skate Stage*!" says John.

Eric says, "They're coming here to Bayview Park. That's great!"

"Wow, Jake Montoya!" says Yoko. "He's the number one skateboarder in the world!"

Eric says, "Let's go. Let's go and buy the tickets today."

It is the big day! Jake Montoya's men and their truck come. The men make the skate stage.

"Look at that," says John. He's looking at the skate stage. "I want to skate on that."

Yoko says, "I want a skate park like this here in Bayview."

"But where's Jake Montoya?" asks John.

Yoko says, "I don't know."

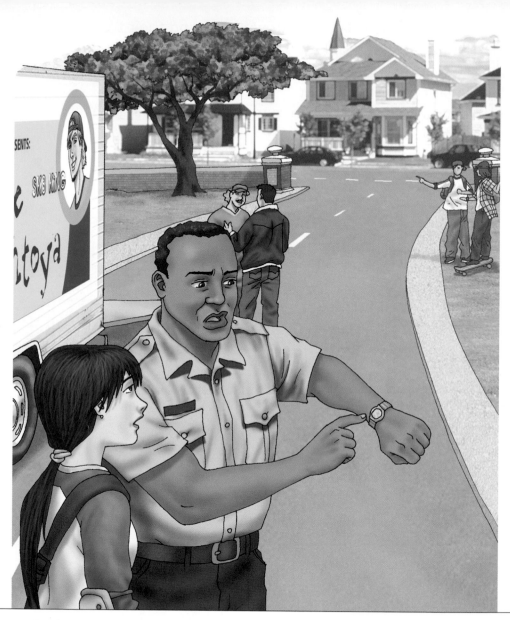

Yoko asks Mr. Walker, "Where's Jake Montoya? Is he here?"
Mr. Walker says, "No. He's late. The show starts at one o'clock."
They look up the street. They do not see Jake.
"Look at the time," says Mr. Walker. "Where is he?"
Mr. Walker is not happy. He is worried. Jake is late.

A man is talking on the phone.
"Oh no!" he says. "Really? Oh, okay. Bye."
"Where's Jake now?" asks his friend.
The man says, "Jake's late. He's coming at two o'clock."
Mr. Walker is listening to the man. Now he is very worried.
Many people have tickets for the show.
"What do I do now?" he thinks.

Yoko and Eric look at the skate stage. It says *Jake Montoya Sk8 Stage*.

"Wow! Look at that," says Yoko. "I like Jake's stage!"

Mr. Walker is listening to them. He knows they are good skateboarders. He has an idea.

Mr. Walker says, "Jake Montoya's late. Do you want to go on Jake Montoya's skate stage?" he asks.

"Oh yes, please," they say. "Yes, please!"

Mr. Walker talks to the man. He tells the man about Eric, Yoko, and John.

Mr. Walker says, "Jake Montoya's late. They want to go on the skate stage. They are very good skateboarders. People can watch them. Is that okay?"

"That's a great idea!" says the man.

Yoko is very excited. "Great! Thanks!" she says.

"Let's go! John, Eric, come on."

They go to the skate stage. They start to skate. Everybody watches them.

"This is great!" says Yoko.

"Yeah," says Eric. "Really great!"

John says, "Watch this!" He jumps very high.

People buy tickets for the *Jake Montoya Show*. Many people buy ice cream and hot dogs, too.

Then Jake Montoya comes to the park.
Yoko sees Jake. "Jake Montoya! Wow. Umm. . . Hi, Mr. Montoya."
"Hi. Call me Jake," he says. "Thanks for helping us."
"You're welcome, Jake," says Eric.
Jake says, "You're very good skateboarders!"

"Do you want to skate with me?" asks Jake.
"Yes, please," say Eric and Yoko. They go on the skate stage.
Yoko, Eric, and John are very excited. They are skating with
Jake Montoya! They have a great time with Jake. He shows
them many things. Everybody is very happy.

"Thanks for the show, Jake," says Mr. Walker. "Really great."
"Thanks again, everybody. You're really good skateboarders," says Jake. "Here are some T-shirts for you."
John says, "Wow! Thanks, Jake!"
"I want to say thank you, too," thinks Mr. Walker. He has an idea.

Four weeks later, John, Eric, and Yoko come to Bayview
Park. There is a new skate park.
Eric says, "Wow, look at that!"
"This is for you and your friends," says Mr. Walker to Yoko.
"Thanks, Mr. Walker," says Yoko.
John says, "Let's go, everybody!"
"I want to try, too," says Mr. Walker.